COME FORTH

A Collection of Poetic Insights,
Prayers & Testimonies to Encourage
the Body of Christ

Taylur Holland

COME FORTH

A Collection of Poetic Insights, Prayers & Testimonies to Encourage the Body of Christ

Copyright © 2016 by Taylur Holland

Cover and layout design, editing, book coaching, and self-publishing services provided by KishKnows, Inc., Richton Park, Illinois, 708-252-DOIT
admin@kishknows.com, www.kishknows.com

ISBN 978-0-692-78419-8
LCCN 2016915664

Scripture quotations marked (NIV) are taken from the Holy Bible, New International Version®, NIV®. Copyright © 1973, 1978, 1984, 2011 by Biblica, Inc.™ Used by permission of Zondervan. All rights reserved worldwide. www.zondervan.com The "NIV" and "New International Version" are trademarks registered in the United States Patent and Trademark Office by Biblica, Inc.™

Scripture quotations marked (NKJV) are taken from the New King James Version®. Copyright © 1982 by Thomas Nelson. Used by permission. All rights reserved.

All rights reserved. No part of this book may be reproduced or transmitted in any form or by any means without written permission from the author.

Printed in the United States of America

Look Whose Talking About..........
COME FORTH

I highly recommend this book! From the initial poem, "Prophetic Poets Arise," I was captured. This is more than a book of poems; it's truly a book of God's heart. The author scribes in detail, bringing her audience into the very words declared. This book speaks to those inside and outside the walls of the church. It's encouraging, motivating, uplifting, and inspiring. Reading this book you will discover the heart of God. The author uses personality, charisma, and style to deliver each poem. The words were well thought, and it's evident she has the pen of a ready writer. As one will read the book of Psalms for poetry, I would couple it with this book as a daily devotion.
~ Sophia Ruffin, Ambassador/Author, Sophia Ruffin Ministries, Chicago Heights, IL

The "U" is for UNIQUE! Taylur "With a U" Holland's *Come Forth* is a literary hybrid in a class of its own! The book is hardly just a collection of poetry, but more like a series of short life-stories that tackle everything from love, to gossip, racism, and destiny, all written through the lens of faith.

Taylur's style of writing provokes the soul to restlessness and arrests the spirit to change. The words of *Come Forth* are compelling, persuasive, and uniquely woven through the breath of God. Breathe in these words of life and Come Forth.
~ Lola Cabaya, Founder & Creative Director of thesmokingprophet.com, Monroe, NC

Refreshing, Reviving, Relevant, and Real are just a few words to describe both Taylur and her poetry. As believers navigate through the pages of this poetic masterpiece they will be convinced to take on life with a new perspective and their call of God with a greater commitment.

~ Dr. Kisia L. Coleman, M.O.D.E.L. (Mentoring Our Daughters, Equipping Ladies) Ministries Founder, Kingdom Church International, Co-Senior Pastor

Dedication

Tears sting my eyes when I think of you.
I just miss you,
And in missing you,
I am discovering that life should be treasured,
That it should be lived and enjoyed,
That life should be so intertwined with Fearless
That not even Eternity can rend the two apart.
You lived,
And you were unafraid.
Sixty-five years, and you lived every moment.
Your example is what I have left,
And here I am now, standing at the edge.
Destiny calls for me,
And Faith longs for me to step out,
To move with reverence
And go after the promise,
To move, to prepare, to leap with expectation,
To live, knowing He is my God –
Forever with me –
The One who equipped me with the grace and access
to do His will in the earth,
To reach the harvest He has given me.
Grandma, you lived,
You leaped,
You were unafraid,
And I thank God for your example.
Destiny is calling for me,

And my heart's response is,
"Here I am Lord.
Here I am.
I am coming forth
As You have called me.
I love You, and I trust You.
You are worth it Lord, so here I am.
You are so worth it, so here I am."

Sons and Daughters, COME FORTH.

This book is dedicated to my grandmother, Judy Marie Cooks.

Table of Contents

LOOK WHOSE TALKING ABOUT	i
DEDICATION	- 1 -
PROPHETIC POETS ARISE!	- 5 -
MY REASON	- 6 -
SHIELD	- 7 -
WILL YOU INVITE ME IN?	- 9 -
JOY AND GLADNESS	- 10 -
BECAUSE OF YOU	- 11 -
TESTIMONY	- 12 -
WRITTEN TREASURES	- 13 -
BRIDGE THE GAP	- 14 -
THE ROOTS OF CONVERSATION	- 16 -
FOREVER YOURS	- 18 -
FAITH OR FEAR	- 19 -
SCHISM	- 20 -
WHEN MY PEN BOWS	- 21 -
IWRITE	- 23 -
WHITE NOISE	- 25 -
ERUPT WITH GLADNESS	- 27 -
VESSEL	- 28 -

DETACHED	- 29 -
FAST-PACED TONGUE	- 30 -
THE GATEKEEPER	- 32 -
FIGHT	- 33 -
WILDERNESS	- 34 -
WHAT ARE YOU DOING WITH THE TIME?.	- 35 -
MORE OF YOU	- 36 -
NOW	- 37 -
IMMEASURABLE	- 39 -
14	- 41 -
WELLS FILLED WITH DUST	- 43 -
SWEET WORDS	- 45 -
WHEN THE U IS FOR UNIQUE	- 48 -
NOTE TO SELF	- 50 -
DEAR TIME	- 51 -
MAY HE SING OVER YOU	- 53 -
THE REST OF THE REMNANT	- 54 -
COME FORTH	- 57 -
ACKNOWLEDGEMENTS	- 58 -
MEET THE AUTHOR	- 60 -

Prophetic Poets Arise!

Prophetic poets, arise at the beckoning of the Father's heart —
His heart — the sound of a trumpet declaring that your time has come.
Arise and see.
Arise and pen the truths that are ready to be fulfilled,
The songs that are ready to be sung.
You have been enveloped, cloaked for a time such as this....
Set apart for reasons that Time will dictate when she is permitted to find her voice.
You have been given grace to write His vision and make it plain.
Scribe,
Poet,
Wordsmith,
Prophet...
Write and declare the testimony of Jesus Christ!

#PropheticPoetsArise

My Reason

HE is my reason for rejoicing,
My reason for singing,
My reason for praising,
My reason for dancing.
Without Him, I drift,
And without Him I am blind.
HE is my Covering and my Protection —
The Lord is my Peace of Mind.
HE is my Resting Place,
And from Him I cannot stray.
Empty was never enough.
HE has gathered me back from that place.
One word and one touch —
By these my life was changed.
HE has made me whole.
Forever will HE be the reason I praise.

Shield

Let us be a shield
One for another.
Let us cover each other
With words from Heaven's heart.
Let us align and strengthen each other
And encompass each other round about
With God's word,
With His promises, and
With sight of what He has already declared.

Can you see for me?
Can you hear for me?
Can you cover me when I am weak?
Can you recall the word of the Lord,
Prepare it as sustenance for me,
And nourish my memory?

We are one body,
One people, fit together to present the kingdom of the living God again –
Here in the earth, and
Here in this moment.
Let us be a shield
One for another.
Let us cover each other
With words of life and words of wisdom.

Let us cover each other with words from Heaven's heart.

Will You Invite Me In?

There is a weight
That crushes the head of every enemy.
When I am invited in,
The weight of My glory, the weight of My mighty presence
Disrupts and dismantles the stance of the enemy.
I will shake him out of place.
I will remove his protection, displace him, and nullify his plan.
But will you invite Me in?
Will you praise Me with your whole heart?
Will you worship Me?
Will you cry out to Me?
When Earth's chorus joins the chorus of Heaven,
What is it that I cannot do?
What is it that I cannot accomplish?
What is it that I cannot perform?
When Earth moves, Heaven will respond,
And your enemies will be scattered.
They will tremble at the sound of my arrival –
Triumphant and glorious.
Peace.
But will you invite Me in?

Joy and Gladness

Light up my world with Your presence.
You are my Lifeline,
And my Whole.
You are Who and What makes sense
When everything else seems to fade.
With You, with You, I am complete.
With You, I am enough – held precious in Your sight.
It is You that has made me glad,
And I will serve You.
Joy has filled my lungs – so much so
That every breath that comes forth is as a song –
A sweet, melodious surrender to the King on high.
I will sing unto You
And gather to You all my adoration.
I will worship You and adorn You with praises.
I will dance before You and sing unto You a new song.
Father, it is joy and it is gladness
That You are causing me to hear and understand.
I will respond to their voices
And be enveloped in their splendor.
With them, will I rejoice and find my delight in You.
With joy and with gladness, will I find my delight in You.

Because of You

Lord, You are my strength and my identity.
You make me to rise and not fail.
You make me to begin again and walk anew.
You are my peace in the morning hour
And my grace in the night.
Without You, I am lost,
And apart from You, I do nothing.
My flesh and my heart may fail
But it is You, God, who is the strength of my heart
and my portion forever.
With You, by You, and through You,
Do I live.

Testimony

I have been compelled to tell a story.
I have been compelled to tell the story of the freed man.
No longer captive.
No longer wandering.
Free and with purpose intact.
I am here to give him a voice,
Write his story,
And sing his song.
His melody is unchained,
And his prison door has been shaken loose from its hinges.
Walk, free man.
Walk in Him that re-membered you,
Put you together again, and breathed His breath into your lungs.
He wanted you to live because He wanted to live through you.
He had to awaken you from slumber
And seep life into your brittle bones —
Yet, He is your strength
And your Redeemer.
I have been commissioned to tell your story —
Compelled to tell it again and again,
Until my very last breath.

Written Treasures

With your pen, unearth
written treasures buried deep
in the midst of you.

Bridge the Gap

Running neck and neck
With yesteryear's breath
Trying to figure out how to stay in your glory –
So afraid of losing territory,
And the new gaining ground.

Running neck and neck
With yesteryear's breath
Trying to figure out how to stay in your glory –
Afraid of losing territory,
You refuse to bridge the gap.

Old needs new,
And new needs old.
We can't separate the two.
Perfect balance, no unjust scales.
Each side, a spoken reflection of the other's tale.

Old man, be willing to teach.
Young man, be willing to learn.

Old man, understand and remember your fervor.
Young man, take heed to legacy and the foundation
of experience.

Old man, be willing to give.
Young man, be willing to accept wise counsel.

Old man, we will not forget you.
Young man, remember the path the old man tread
and let it guide you.

The Roots of Conversation

Steaming cup
On square table with rounded edges.
Light comes through kitchen's window.
Morning.

Chatter dances atop the air in this room
And fills the room with its (e)motions until they can no longer fit
And must spill into the next room to cut its rugs up too.
Conversation.

What are the words?
Are the babblings vain?
Is the speech corrupt?
Are the words overlaid with the indiscriminate cloak of gossip?
Are they frayed with Complaint and Murmur?
Have the words been kissed by Death before whizzing through kitchen's window to go murder the character of your brother or sister
Then ransack their home?
Questions.

Words.
Where do their roots begin?

Words.
Where are they found?
Question.

Have you considered your thoughts?

Forever Yours

I will not be moved out of place
Because You, Lord, are my saving grace,
And I will keep my face
Set as a flint.
Lord, You give me strength
To walk each day,
To war and to stand,
And from You, never look away.
You are my captain,
My source,
And my peace of mind.
You are my illumination,
For God, You are my light.
You transferred me from darkness' kingdom and
Into Yours.
You made me whole.
You are my source.
You are my joy,
And my forevermore.
You are the song that I sing,
So sweet and so loving.
Oh tender One,
Thank You for being all of my joy.
Thank You for being all of my source.
You claimed me before my very first breath.
Father, I am forever Yours.

Faith or Fear

With every step we
must choose to serve faith or fear —
which master will rule?

Schism

Racism,
a demonic schism
that has pushed many aside
and cast them, like prisoners, into pits
built with jagged colored lines.

Racism,
a demonic stronghold
which seeks to maintain the great divide
by portraying lies as truth and
reiterating the fable that there peacefully can be no
me and you.

Racism
has left this nation devoid of peace —
no justice has run to the forefront and life
carries on with stringent ease as
we look for the next rug our broom should meet.

Racism.

When My Pen Bows

You have put Your words in my pen. When my pen bows before You, the sound and handwriting of Your heart fills the page that lays at Your feet.

My ear.

How sweet is the portion of Your words that You give to me. How sweet is the melodious flow of Your written mind from Your throne and right into my ear.

The page.

When my pen bows before You, she is not hurried away but longs to stay in Your presence. When she bows, she kisses Your feet and begins to sing unto You. Boldly — and with full assurance that You hear her. She loves You and longs for You. She loves for You to fill her with words, and her steady pursuit is of You alone. She waits for You. She waits for the time when You allow her to release Your thoughts. She is glad when You share them with her. With such joy she bows — unceasingly waiting with ecstasy. Oh how she loves You, and quickly she pours out the words of Your heart onto the page laid at Your feet.

My ear.

Oh how this page loves to carry the stories of Your heart.

iWrite

I don't write pages for reactions.
I write to restore hope.
I write to fight.
I write to remind you that you are His —
The King's kid —
And who He is
Is far beyond those who hurt and abandoned you.
I write to hold up the looking glass.
Peer deep and see that no one can be you
But you.
I write to unearth the key —
The key that will unlock the fetters
From around your wrists and feet
And set you free.
I write to help you witness peace
And restoration.
Get reacquainted with them both,
And with the revelation of redemption.
Run right to His throne.
I write because I believe that through the words I'm given
Someone will see Christ —
The One we so desperately need.
The world cries, "Show me Jesus!"
So my heart is for these words to frame His image
Show how beautiful He is and just how splendid
Is His majesty.

I want people to be made whole,
And get to know the Creator as Father.
Perfect in all His ways,
But not so far away that He cannot save.
He is near you.
Don't fret.
Find Him in the midst of your very breath.
Find Him as a new day begins to beckon in your depth —
Miracle.
Find Him.
See Him.
Let Him make you whole.
I write,
And I wrote this poem
For you to see Hope —
He Who has kept you and loved you all along.

White Noise

Finding sounds
Rewritten in crowds
Having to hear past the thick
And contend with the blocks
That wish to intercept the voice of promise.

Hold fast to the Shepherd's voice and don't fret.
Wait for Him
Because He's not done with you yet.

This is the season to push, press, and persist.
This is the time to not give up in prayer
And the waning, you must resist.

Don't be afraid of the hand of the enemy,
For God has equipped
You with all life and godliness.
Therefore, you have the ability
To overcome
Because it is He that is with you.
He is your light, your salvation, and your strength —
No need to be afraid or revere some
One or something above Him.
He is King —
The perfect One who sees
All.
He — so acquainted with your end,

Trust Him, and know that it is in Him that you are
safely hid —
So high up, you cannot be touched
Or accessed by any enemy.
You are covered in the blood
So you have the victory!

Hear past the white noise.
Hear through to your deliverance.
Your peace is found in His voice.
So if God be for you, then who can be against
You and stand?

Erupt With Gladness

Erupt with gladness
In this day,
And know that your peace is not far off.
Sing with joy everlasting,
And hope to no end.
Keep your eyes to the mountains
Because from there your help will surely come.
Don't get discouraged
And become dismayed,
But know that He has made your path straight.
Do not be aligned with wrong thought-patterns and ideas,
Believe them in your heart,
Then confess their lies as truth.
But speak life and be undeterred.
Speak that which heaven has already declared about you.
Erupt with gladness
In this day,
And know that your peace is not far off.

Vessel

I am everything that you need.
You were broken to be opened,
So that you could be filled by Me.
So don't be afraid of what has happened,
For I am the captain of your soul.
I'm your lover and your friend,
Your King —
Everything that you need.

You are My vessel,
My son,
My daughter,
My treasure.
None of your experiences have been wasted, and
You are not tainted.
Through it all,
I was with you,
And even now, I walk with you.

You are Mine, and
I am Yours.
Abide in Me,
And I in You….
I am all that you need.
So know, My vessel —
My child —
That you were broken to be opened
So that you could be filled by Me.

Detached

Detached.
The status of many hearts.
Leaders detached from Father God.
The people detached from Him as well.
No relationship outside of the four walls.
No connection beyond the gathering of souls
To view screens.
Sit in seats —
No interaction.
No movement.
No involvement.
Just come and sit,
And look and leave.
Convenience.
Go into this building,
Hear a message that's sweet, and
Then leave through the same door.
No change required.

There has to be more.

Fast-Paced Tongue

Fast-paced tongue
Jumping the gun
Too quick —
Missing the mark
Ready to jump the hurdles
Called discernment.

Every time, you're ready to run all in.
Slowing down only relays
The message of ancient,
And that you'll miss something
If you don't move quick.

Pass the baton,
Lap done,
Then go and pick up another one.
Milestones you're reaching with heat,
And when things go south
These same stones you throw with ease.

No restraint as you maintain a swift pace
To outrun Time,
But you don't comprehend longevity
And what it means to give it time.

That is too long of a jump,
Just too much distance, and you'd

Rather go high than be confined
To red flags
That point you to the other direction.

You are selective in what you see,
And in what you believe.
So, your breath
Curses Time
Whenever it pushes to contest
What you want
And who you deem as fitting.

Fast-paced tongue
Jumping the gun
Too quick —
Missing the mark
Every time you refuse discernment.

The Gatekeeper

The gatekeeper's job
is to ward off intruders —
ruin – if he sleeps.

Fight

Two-toned clouds —
Split between beams of light on one side,
And undergirded by darkness on the other.
The word of promise has been decreed
And declared.
Trumpets have announced the coming of light,
And darkness has perched his ear to hear.
He has cast his net wide to intercept the word and swallow it whole.
And you are in the midst,
Standing in between promise and calamity.
The wind of God has blown to signal your changing season,
And the enemy's gust rushes in to shake the ground beneath your feet.
Words swirl round about —
God's voice,
The enemy's voice,
Your voice.
What do you do?

Fight.

Timothy, my son, I am giving you this command in keeping with the prophecies once made about you, so that by recalling them you may fight the battle well.
1 Timothy 1:18 (NIV)

Wilderness

Your praise will possess
the promise, so don't curse and
forsake the process.

What Are You Doing with the Time?

i thought time would wake me up,
roll me out from under the covers of stagnation
and scream, "WAKE UP!" — but she didn't.
she let me sleep,
unconscious and losing territory —
defenses dismantled and grounds left open for the enemy to camp.
no gatekeeper.
i wonder if time wept for me.
did she cry when i closed my eyes to her again and again?
was she saddened every time i sank deeper into the abyss of "one day"
and made my bed in the mouth of delay?
i…i just wonder.

More of You

More of You is required
Because it is only You who can sustain me.
More of You is required
Because this longing for You is deep.
In Your presence, God, I reside with Peace.
In Your presence, Lord, I dance with Joy.
In Your presence, I am wrapped with Gladness.
In Your presence, I sing a new song.
You make me whole.
You cause me to live.
I just want You,
And to know that You want me too is life everlasting.
Father, thank You for Your mercy and
lovingkindness.
Thank You for Your presence.
Whom have I in heaven but You?
And there is none upon earth that I desire beside You.
Fill me up Lord.
I need more of You.

Now

Even tears are seeds.
Prayers sown
In grounds and places awaiting breakthrough.
The land has opened wide its mouth
For the presence of the Lord to fill it —
Gulping and gasping for the breath of God.
The land bulges itself out to make room and to make ready to receive
And to receive again.
Your people are crying out.
We want to see You move.
We want to see Your hand.
We want to see Your glory all over the earth,
Kingly manifestations of power that will turn hearts back to the remembrance of You.
Revival.
Our hearts' desire.
Revival.
To know You once more,
To be carried in the folds of Your garment.
Jesus, we don't want just parts of You.
We want the whole of You.
Jesus, sing unto us.
Sing over us Your song
Which glorifies the Father,
The Most High.
Beautiful.

Enrich us with Your power,
And fill us with the fear of You.
Sovereign God, we are crying out,
Longing to be saved,
Longing to adorn You with the jewels of our worship.
We honor You.
We honor You.
We honor You.
There is a generation that won't be quiet about the things of God —
A generation that will reverence You, Father,
And only do what pleases You.
There is a generation,
And we are now.

Immeasurable

The weight of man's intellect
Is not enough to measure You.
We cannot contain the whole of You.
Though we try to hold You to four walls,
Who You are cannot be held in the depth of human hands.
You are not defined by a denomination
Or by a checklist of ideas.
You are God,
And the weight of Your glory
Is immeasurable.
To bow in Your presence,
For Your love to sweep over us —
Heaven on earth.
For Your refreshing to fall like rain,
And Your fire to consume us
And we not be destroyed —
Heaven on earth.
King, You are immeasurable.
Your expanse is great, infinite, and not
Marked by the ears of men.
You are found in every corner of the earth,
And it is Your breath that has shaped the winds —
Given them direction and purpose.
God, Your wholeness cannot be understood,
For the strength of man's intellect is not enough to measure You.

You, oh Lord —
Holy,
Beautiful,
Majestic,
Glorious —
Are immeasurable.

14

At fourteen, I found
my voice in poetry.
She was hidden
amongst a beach of white
rocks and an overcast sky
in November.
I called that place
the rock of all ages.

Words.

They became my best
friends.
I would talk to them
in class when history lessons
bored me.
I would rather observe classmates
and write their stories.

Words.

Since I couldn't paint, sketch, or sculpt,
I would strive to construct
pictures with them —
write a vivid photograph,
scribe a colorful image,
pen a portrait

that would help people see what
I saw when I looked at them —
purpose.

Words.

At fourteen, without
map or compass, words
bridged me to Him.

Words.

At fourteen, words saved
my life.

Wells Filled With Dust

stagnant waters.
stale and unmoving.
what appears to be a place of refreshing
is a habitation for flies.
yet, many still come to drink from these wells
filled with dust.

the Presence once made His home in this place,
but when the value of position outranked praise,
suffocated the depth of worship, and arrested
the heart of prayer,
He departed.
they didn't want Him.
yet, many still come to this place to offer adoration
to hollow idols
and drink from these wells
filled with dust.

this place, once a holy temple, is now
a template for many that view it as a steeple of
success.
its image has been replicated time and time again
from its end,
so Glory has never been invited in to take a seat
alongside any of this place's bastard offspring.
yet, many come to drink from these wells
filled with dust.

this place has been built on
the faulty foundation of sweet words
that strive to never highlight the bitterness of sin
that is coiled tight around the torso of every hearer.
constricted and confined, but content — the hearers,
they know no difference and
they look no different
than the world they go to minister to
with cookie cutter scripts in hand.
yes, they want others to come and drink
from these wells
filled with dust.

this dust — the finest there is —
created from what flows out of
the world's broken heart —
the lust of the flesh,
the lust of the eyes,
and the pride of life.
these have crept into this place —
once a holy temple —
and many run to drink from its wells
filled with dust
simply because
they're just so used to doing it.

Sweet Words

When focus wasn't sure, you painted a picture.
You created a world that spoke nothing,
Yet solidified your wandering.
You wanted to live freely,
Yield to no one.
So you created a world.

Colors flew all about.
You danced amongst blades of grass
And grazed your hands over pools of flowers.
The light you constructed never dimmed,
And the darkness from truth
Was never allowed to stand in your place.
You wanted to keep living in this fairy tale, so
Conviction was not permitted.

Your ears were turned away from correction.
Stroke after stroke,
Rigid brush after rigid brush,
Fix this, fix that.
"There! Some guilt is seeping through the cracks! —
No! Some desire for wholeness is attempting to ooze through!"
Erase, erase erase.
Erase this wall — Erect another.
Run, run, run,
And don't look back.

You and your world have been running
On the fumes of sweet words, and
They are proving to not be enough.

Change a color here!
Change a color there!
Rewrite the painter's name at the bottom of the page
to
See if you can pronounce it differently
And then maybe the void will be filled.

When vision was skewed, you filled your ears with sweet words….
Sweet nothings that told you, you were alright.
You reached for shepherds that would lead you to
that place — the capital of Astray — better known as,
"You're Okay."
You looked for who would whisper lies and spare
you from Truth —
Him — who you and they did not know.
You wanted your ears tickled with smooth words….

These words, when unbalanced, are barbaric in nature
Because they run out.
They are temporary, and they leave you
Stranded.
Stroke after stroke,
Rigid brush after rigid brush.

Rewrite the painter's name at the bottom of the page
to
See if you can pronounce "Empty"
Any differently.

When the U is for Unique

Unusual.
Unafraid to Unapologetically be me.
I need the U to spell me.
I need the You to spell me.
I need the You to spell me.

Unadulterated joy I have
Knowing Him.
I am made whole Under the Umbrella of His timing,
Uncovered only when He lifts the lid of
Uncommon favor.

I have always been atypical.
Not your Usual in any way or facet.
It is me that He has fastened to the tip of His pen,
The tip of His tongue and breathed in me an
Unparalleled joy to write again.

I am Unbiased when it comes to the winds of
His love because He moves me,
Swoons me, and soothes me,
Unselfish in His gaze.

I am His,
And He Uniquely made
Me, so there is just no other way
To be.

Just be who He
Made you to be, and
Remember, the YOU
Is always for Unique.

Note to Self

Dear Me,

Sometimes you need to be moving in order to feel the wind, moving without fear and hesitation. Sometimes, you've just got to go forward and trust that the Spirit has gone before you – that He walks alongside you even now. He has equipped you and empowered you to complete the vision. Move, and feel the wind.

Sincerely,

Me

Dear Time

Dear Time,
You and I — we
Go back and forth.
Remember when I told you
That I could beat you in a race?
You just looked at me with steady face,
Cool breath, and stable hands
And shrugged.
I took it as a challenge, and spent you —
Wasted you — trying to overcome you.
You stayed still — it seemed, but really
You were just chill
And steady,
So content in your purpose and comfortable
In your identity,
Unshaken and unmoved by my antics
Because you knew I wasn't ready
For those things that I longed for.
You told me over and over to
Learn to rest in the wait,
To seek His kingdom first.
You told me that in His presence, I would find the
fullness of joy — and
That His joy was my strength — the
Strength I needed to bear the weight of the wait,
To bear the pain of being braided together with Him.
Time, sometimes you and I still don't get along.

We argue like brother and sister, but you're still my best friend.
You love me enough to not let me get ahead of myself.
God chose you to carry my best interests in hand,
And you bear them up with the greatest care
Until Father leads you to meet with Appointed and Due Season
And you lay the promises down at their feet.
You are a faithful steward, and I long
To be more like you:
Patient.
Content in purpose.
Comfortable in identity.
Unshaken and unmoved by the antics of others.
Focused only on doing the will of the Father.
Time,
I long to be more like you.

May He Sing Over You

May He sing over you,
A sweet song of love and life.
May He be the song that is
There waiting for you when you wake up.
May His melody consume you
Before the day's checklist of thoughts attempt to dismantle you.
May His song war on your behalf
And give you peace.
May His song fill you with His thoughts,
His wisdom, and His instructions.
May you be filled with joy at the knowledge and understanding of His compassions.
May you know peace
As He drapes His new mercies over you.
May you know that He is the Lord, your Shepherd, and your King —
And that it is you, in whom He is well pleased.
May He sing a sweet song over you,
A song of life and love eternal.

The Rest of the Remnant

God, thank You for resting
On Your remnant.
Thank You for preparing Your people,
This people who are not forgotten,
This people who will not be swayed.

You, who I have hidden in caves,
In the mountains,
In the wilderness,
I have not forgotten you.
I have not forsaken you,
But I have been building you up
For a time such as this,
Preparing you before Time
Caught wind of placement and learned to bow
Before Eternity.
I am He.
Glorious.

Do not weary in well-doing.
Do not tremble before them.
Do not fret,
But go forth boldly
And proclaim My holiness,
My justice,
My name.
Break free from all that is against you,

And depart from all that will bar you
From holiness,
Purification,
And sanctification.

I am He
That holds you,
That knows you,
That gives you rest.

I am healing the land even now.
I have heard you.
I have heard your cries.
My word runs swiftly,
And it shall prevail.
It will not tarry,
Nor will it be mocked,
But it shall be performed.
Suddenly.
Unexpectedly.
Without hesitation
It shall come to pass.
All of this that I have been
Working out on your behalf –
All of it shall come to pass.
Go in My strength,
And speak in My name.

My remnant.

I love you,
And I have not forgotten you.
You are My joy and My delight.
My chosen.
Hold fast to Me,
And you will not be moved out of place.
I got you.
I have you.
You are Mine.

God, thank You for resting upon the remnant.

Come Forth

Transparency shatters the glass that would seek to keep you concealed,
That would seek to keep you quiet,
Shuttering in the darkness of Secret, and in the depth of swollen tongue.

May you come forth and speak what the Lord has done.
May you come forth, unafraid to open your mouth and tell the unadulterated truth.
Come forth, and come forth boldly.

Yes, come forth.

Acknowledgements

I would like to thank all of those who have encouraged me, strengthened me, and prayed for me during this journey of completing and publishing my very first book. I thank God for sending you into my life to help push me towards purpose and the fulfillment of a dream. I love you all.

To my parents, Dwaylyn and Lujuanne Holland, I love you. Thank you for supporting me and encouraging me to leap forward. Thank you for all the Godly wisdom and insight you pour into my life everyday. I am so blessed to call you Mama and Daddy. Always know, "I'm so proud for you." :)

Dwaylyn II (aka Debo), little big brother, thank you. You are a man of great wisdom and courage. I thank you for always believing in me. You don't let me quit. It is my joy to make you laugh, and I love you. Thank you for inspiring me. Bailey, sister and queen, thank you. I love how God uses you to boldly speak and declare His wisdom. You teach me. You keep me grounded and humble. You protect my heart. Thank you for always being fearless and encouraging me to live life whole - to go after what I want, undeterred and unafraid. You are a blessing, and I love you so much Bay Bay. Jimiah, baby brother who is way bigger than me, thank you. You will forever be my little guy. I cherish you and the amazing young man you are becoming. You are full of His wisdom and His Spirit, and I am so blessed to learn from you. I love you Punkee. Always.

To KishKnows, Inc., thank you. Thank you for being a strength and a help to me during this process. Thank you for working diligently to see this book through to its end. I am grateful for your creativity, your wisdom, sound knowledge, and utter willingness to serve. It has been a pleasure working with you.

To the reader, thank you for purchasing this book. I pray these words bring strength and refreshing to your soul. I pray you are encouraged to press forward in God and stirred to do all that He has called you to do.

Yet now be strong, Zerubbabel,' says the Lord; 'and be strong, Joshua, son of Jehozadak, the high priest; and be strong, all you people of the land,' says the Lord, 'and work; for I am with you,' says the Lord of hosts. 'According to the word that I covenanted with you when you came out of Egypt, so My Spirit remains among you; do not fear!'
Haggai 2:4-5, (NKJV)

Meet the Author

Taylur Holland is a spoken word poet with the anointing of the scribe on her life. She started writing poetry at fourteen years old and since that time God has been speaking both to and through her. It is her heart's desire for people to know peace, healing, answers, and restoration when they experience her writings.

Taylur is a consultant in the finance industry and a graduate of Texas A & M University with a Bachelor's of Business Administration in Finance. She resides in Mesquite, Texas, and when she is not writing, Taylur enjoys spending time with her family and friends, drinking coffee or bubble tea, reading, and listening to music.

For booking information or inquiries please visit: www.thescribesheart.com

www.ingramcontent.com/pod-product-compliance
Lightning Source LLC
Chambersburg PA
CBHW072109290426
44110CB00014B/1875